W9-BAT-439

HEADLINES!™

AMERICA'S RECESSION

THE EFFECTS OF THE ECONOMIC DOWNTURN

CORONA BREZINA

ROSEN
PUBLISHING®

New York

Published in 2011 by The Rosen Publishing Group, Inc.
29 East 21st Street, New York, NY 10010

First Edition

Library of Congress Cataloging-in-Publication Data

Brezina, Corona.
America's recession: the effects of the economic downturn / Corona Brezina.
    p. cm. — (Headlines!)
Includes bibliographical references and index.
ISBN 978-1-4488-1296-7 (library binding)
1. United States—Economic conditions—2009—Juvenile literature.
2. United States—Economic policy—2009—Juvenile literature.
3. Recessions—United States—Juvenile literature.
4. Global financial crisis, 2008–2009—Juvenile literature. I. Title.
HC106.84.B74 2011
330.973—dc22

2010016915

Manufactured in Malaysia

CPSIA Compliance Information: Batch #W11YA: For further information, contact Rosen Publishing, New York, New York, at 1-800-237-9932.

On the cover: On August 9, 2007, a trader on the floor of the New York Stock Exchange reacts to plummeting stock market prices.

CONTENTS

I n December 2007, the United States entered a crippling economic recession. The root cause of the recession was the 2006 collapse of the country's housing market, which caused a credit crisis affecting the entire world's economy. The global recession was the worst economic downturn in the United States since the Great Depression, which lasted from 1929 to 1934. Many observers began calling the new global recession the "Great Recession."

Few economists had anticipated the severity of the Great Recession. During the fall of 2008, the financial crisis dominated headlines. Hard times began to hit ordinary Americans.

During late 2008 and early 2009, hundreds of thousands of jobs were lost every month. Unemployment rates increased to levels not seen for decades. Foreclosure rates soared, as home-owners were unable to pay their monthly mortgages and had their homes repossessed by banks as a result.

Even as the economy entered a period of recovery in late 2009, many Americans remained pessimistic. The recession had cost people their jobs and their savings. The unemployment rate remained high. Employers were not hiring new workers. Ordinary Americans worried about their financial security.

President Barack Obama tours Industrial Support Inc., a Buffalo, New York, manufacturing company, in 2010. Obama was in Buffalo to deliver a speech about federal economic recovery efforts.

CHAPTER 1
ROOTS OF THE RECESSION

America's recession, which officially began in December 2007, had its roots in the 2006 collapse of the U.S. housing market. Just prior to this collapse, the housing market had been thriving. The prices of homes and other properties were rapidly increasing. When a real estate agent listed a house on the market, it usually sold quickly and at a good price. Potential buyers viewing a home for sale sometimes took along their checkbooks so that they could act quickly if they wanted to buy. If they didn't buy immediately, there was a chance that someone else might make an offer before they had a chance.

People upgraded to bigger houses, and many Americans became homeowners for the first time. Banks introduced new loan programs that made it easier for people to become homebuyers. Borrowers did not always have to show that they had a steady income in order to get a loan, and they were not always required to make a substantial down payment when purchasing a home.

Because these loans were made available to borrowers who may not have qualified for a traditional mortgage, they were called sub-prime mortgages. New homeowners often did not pay attention to

BREAKING NEWS • BREAKING NEWS • BREAKING NEWS • BREAKING NEWS • BREAKING NEWS • BREAKIN

A job seeker looks over employment postings in November 2008 as jobless numbers increased to the highest level in twenty-five years.

the terms of these mortgages. Many subprime mortgages featured variable interest rates. Variable interest rates might start out low, but they could greatly increase after a year or two.

THE PEAK OF THE HOUSING BOOM

Banks stood to make huge profits from the housing market. They began repackaging mortgages—splitting them up, combining them with other types of debt, and selling them to investors. Financial firms bought and traded repackaged mortgages on the market. Trading repackaged mortgages became a huge business worth trillions of dollars. As home values grew and banks issued more mortgages, financial firms saw their profits grow. Banks began borrowing far more money than they actually possessed. Some banks owed $30 in debt for every dollar they held. Although these deals and practices were very profitable, they were also very risky.

In 2005, the housing market was thriving, and homeowners saw the value of their property rising. Many people saw this as an opportunity to trade some of this value in for cash. They took out new mortgages on their homes, which banks were happy to grant.

This was the peak of the housing boom, however, and it could not last forever. Soon, home prices began to fall. New homes stood vacant, and sellers were unable to find buyers. Borrowers began to default on their mortgages, which means that they failed to make their monthly payments.

THE ECONOMIC DOWNTURN BEGINS

The economy had been booming during the early 2000s, but many American consumers were in debt. People took on mortgages, car loans, credit card debt, and student loans. When they were unable to repay these debts, it had a negative effect on the financial markets. By 2007, investment banks were losing money on risky business ventures based on subprime loans. It became clear that the collapse of the housing market was going to lead to hard times.

Americans were feeling pressure in other economic areas as well. In 2008, the prices of commodities such as oil, food, and raw materials began to rise. A barrel of oil cost about $30 in 2003. By July 2008, the price had skyrocketed to a record high of more than $147. Oil companies such as Exxon Mobil saw record-breaking profits, and observers warned the public that the United States was entering a new era of high energy prices. After the global recession hit, however, commodity prices declined.

Politicians and economists began to recognize the likelihood of an economic downturn occurring. President George W. Bush signed the American Stimulus Act of 2008 in February of that year. The act

A driver fills up his SUV in 2008. During the recession, rising oil prices caused gas prices to soar.

was intended to prevent or relieve the effects of a possible recession. The main feature of the $150 billion plan was a tax rebate check sent to about 130 million Americans. The administration believed that this spending boost would stimulate the faltering economy. Ultimately, the act was not adequate to reverse the recession.

THE FINANCIAL CRISIS

Throughout the spring and summer of 2008, there were signs of a deepening credit crisis in the financial industry. Banks were unwilling

THE BUSINESS CYCLE

Recessions are a normal part of the business cycle, which consists of alternating periods of economic growth and contraction. The business cycle represents changes in the economy's gross domestic product, the measure of the value of all of the goods and services produced in a nation. There are four phases in the business cycle: peak, recession, trough, and expansion. The peak is the maximum point of economic growth. After the peak is reached, the economy contracts, resulting in a period of recession. The lowest point in the economic downturn is the trough, after which the economy recovers during a period of expansion and renewed growth.

or unable to lend money. In March 2008, the bank JPMorgan Chase acquired Bear Stearns, the fifth largest investment bank on Wall Street, rescuing it from the brink of collapse. After Bear Stearns suffered steep losses due to subprime mortgages, other banks had ceased lending it money. The U.S. government backed the purchase of Bear Stearns. This signaled that the government was willing to rescue financial giants if their collapse could severely impact the economy.

In September 2008, the unease in the financial industry reached a crisis point. On September 8, the government took over Fannie Mae and Freddie Mac, the nation's two largest mortgage holders. A week later, Lehman Brothers, one of Wall Street's biggest investment banks, went bankrupt. The collapse stunned the financial industry. Part of this shock was due to the fact that the U.S. government did not act to rescue Lehman Brothers. This increased the sense of insecurity for other troubled financial institutions.

On September 16, the government bailed out the insurance giant American International Group, Inc. (AIG), which had sustained substantial losses insuring risky investments. During the last week of the month, a major bank, Washington Mutual, failed. Wachovia, another troubled bank, entered negotiations for a takeover by a more stable bank.

The stock market reflected the meltdown in the financial sector. In early October, the Dow Jones Industrial Average experienced its worst losses in history, losing 22 percent of its value over a period of eight days. A year earlier, on October 9, 2007, the Dow had closed at a record high of 14,164. From there, it declined rapidly. Between October 1 and October 10, 2008, the Dow fell from 10,831 to 8,451.

Banks had cut back on lending to each other as investments based on subprime mortgages collapsed. They also cut back on lending to businesses and individuals. It became more difficult and expensive to obtain loans. Businesses could not receive loans for new investments. Individuals could not obtain loans for major purchases such as cars or houses. This had a chilling effect on the overall health of the economy. Although many banks and other financial institutions received bailout money during the fall of 2008, lending was not greatly increased.

GOVERNMENT AID

In late September 2008, Congress began debating legislative measures to confront the financial crisis. Congress's first priority was to restore confidence in the financial markets. This goal marked the beginning of government measures aimed at restoring the nation's economic health.

Members of the Senate Banking Committee talk to reporters in September 2008 during negotiations on a financial bailout package for troubled financial institutions. Seen here are *(left to right)* Massachusetts Senator Barney Frank, Connecticut Senator Chris Dodd, and New York Senator Charles Schumer.

In addition to financial institutions, other industries, most notably the U.S. auto industry, required government aid. Then there were the victims of the recession, such as homeowners in danger of losing their houses and unemployed workers who had lost their jobs.

After the worst of the crisis had passed, lawmakers would begin to debate what kind of financial reforms could prevent such a disaster from occurring again. From the very beginning, government actions involving the financial crisis and recession proved to be controversial.

CHAPTER 2
ADDRESSING THE CRISIS

A s the financial crisis unfolded in the fall of 2008, it became clear that strong government intervention was required. The Federal Reserve, chaired by Ben Bernanke, and the U.S. Treasury Department, headed by Henry Paulson, worked to save failing financial institutions. On September 18, Paulson unveiled a $700 billion proposal for the Troubled Asset Relief Program (TARP). Under TARP, the government would buy troubled assets from struggling banks. This would prevent their collapse and relieve the credit crisis.

The public and many lawmakers reacted with indignation. Some believed that TARP went against the concept of a free market. They believed the fact that these financial institutions required government aid indicated they were not strong enough to compete with other institutions and thus should be allowed to fail. Others objected to the bailouts on the grounds that they constituted a "moral hazard." These people believed the banks had brought about their financial problems through risky business deals. If the government rescued them with public money, this would reward such irresponsible behavior and let the culprits off the hook. Doing so could set a dangerous precedent.

TARP supporters countered that some financial institutions had grown "too big to fail." If they were allowed to collapse, it could

Treasury Secretary Henry Paulson *(right)* heads to the White House on September 18, 2008, to discuss the worsening financial crisis with President George W. Bush.

destabilize the entire financial industry and the industries that rely on it. They believed the potential danger to the national economy outweighed the moral hazard and cost to the public.

Congress amended Paulson's proposal, which was strongly supported by Bush. On September 29, however, the U.S. House of Representatives voted against passing the TARP bill. After further negotiations, the House and the U.S. Senate approved the bill in early October. The Federal Reserve and the Treasury began the first round of bailouts, handing out money to financial institutions and buying investments based on bad mortgages. By accepting TARP funds, banks had to consent to oversight measures, such as limits on executive pay.

CAMPAIGNING THROUGH THE CRISIS

As the financial crisis unfolded and the United States descended deeper into a recession, Republican senator John McCain from

ECONOMIC INDICATORS

In addition to the gross domestic product (GDP), a number of other variables are used to plot economic trends. These are known as economic indicators. Two categories of economic indicators are leading indicators and lagging indicators.

Leading indicators can show economic change before the GDP changes. For this reason, economists use these statistics to predict the direction of the economy. Leading indicators include stock market values, retail sales, unemployment claims, new building permits, and new orders for industrial plants and machinery. If leading indicators are favorable, experts predict that economic growth will follow.

Lagging indicators, on the other hand, are the statistics that change after the GDP changes. If the economy is growing, improvements in lagging indicators will follow later. Lagging indicators include the unemployment rate and the length of time that people remain unemployed.

Economists base their projections on overall economic trends, not individual reports on economic indicators. A one-month upswing in unemployment levels, for example, could just be a fluke. A pattern of improvement across many different indicators over a period of months, however, likely signals economic growth.

Arizona and Democratic senator Barack Obama from Illinois were in the middle of their presidential campaigns. The economy became the dominant issue of the election. Both McCain and Obama supported the TARP plan. On September 24, 2008, McCain announced that he was suspending his election campaign due to the financial meltdown so that he could help negotiate the bailout plan. The move did not help his image as a leader, however. The initial TARP bill was defeated in the House largely due to Republican opposition.

Voters were concerned about the faltering economy and anxious about their own financial security. Although McCain portrayed himself as a "maverick," voters still associated him with the policies of George W. Bush—highly unpopular as the outgoing president—and the Republican leadership. Obama's message of "change" resonated more strongly with voters who were worried about the state of the economy. On November 4, Obama was elected president.

During the period between Obama's election and his inauguration, dire economic news continued to dominate the headlines. Factory orders declined more than expected, and major corporations reported earnings losses. Home sales plummeted, mortgage delinquency increased, and foreclosure numbers soared. Bank bailouts and bank failures continued. Stories about layoffs became a regular feature in the news, and massive monthly job losses pushed unemployment figures to levels not seen for more than a decade. Retail sales declined significantly; some chains of stores, including the electronics giant Circuit City, went bankrupt. The struggling "Big Three" U.S. automakers—General Motors (GM), Chrysler, and Ford—entered contentious negotiations with Congress over government assistance.

On December 1, economists officially announced that the economy was experiencing a recession that had begun a year earlier. The 2008 Christmas shopping season was the worst in decades, with many retailers reporting a huge drop in sales from 2007.

President Barack Obama signs the American Recovery and Reinvestment Act (ARRA) on February 17, 2009.

As he prepared to take office, president-elect Obama assembled his economic team and began crafting plans to combat the recession. Although he urged the outgoing Congress to enact a stimulus plan immediately, it did not come to pass. Obama assured Americans that shoring up the economy would be his first priority upon taking office.

THE STIMULUS PLAN OF 2009

Barack Obama took office as president on January 20, 2009. He had laid out a broad agenda for an economic stimulus plan. The Senate and the House worked out the details and drafted the text of the bill. In the Senate, there was intense negotiation between Democrats and Republicans on the scope and cost of the bill. The bill passed the Senate by a vote of 60–38. Three Republicans voted for the bill. In the House, it passed by a vote of 246–143. Not a single Republican representative voted for the bill. Since the two bills differed in some respects, Obama met with leaders of the House and Senate to negotiate a final version.

Obama signed the finalized bill, called the American Recovery and Reinvestment Act (ARRA) of 2009, on February 17. The total cost was $787 billion, which included $501 billion in spending and $286 billion in tax cuts. Much of the spending was intended to help pay for health care costs, unemployment compensation, education, job training, and food assistance.

Stimulus money was to be distributed over a period of several years to bolster a sustained recovery. Much of this money was directed to the states. The act included spending for public works projects, such as building roads and bridges, which would provide jobs for out-of-work Americans. Spending was also allocated for renewable energy, science and health research, environmental projects, and transportation improvements. The bulk of the tax incentives went to individuals, rather than businesses. In addition to general tax measures, such as a tax credit aimed toward middle-income workers, the act included tax incentives for buying new homes and cars.

The bill received both praise and criticism. Some Democrats claimed that an even larger package was needed to fix the economy. Republicans held that the bill was already much too expensive, dangerously increasing the federal deficit. The bill was also criticized for focusing on spending, rather than job creation.

A year after the implementation of the act, opinions on its success were mixed. In late 2009, government officials admitted that they had underestimated the severity of the economic downturn. The government had projected that the unemployment level would peak at 8.5 percent before beginning to fall. Instead, the unemployment level climbed above 10 percent. Critics pointed to these figures in declaring the stimulus plan a failure. Supporters countered by claiming that the recession would have been far worse without the effects of the stimulus plan.

The stimulus plan saved jobs that would otherwise have been eliminated, especially essential positions such as policemen and teachers. Aid provided by the plan, such as unemployment payments and food assistance, boosts the economy by enabling consumer spending. The stimulus plan helped promote economic growth, and the GDP began increasing in mid-2009.

Some ARRA efforts were more successful than others. During the summer of 2009, the Cash for Clunkers program was introduced. It was intended to boost vehicle sales and help the troubled auto industry. Customers who traded in cars or trucks for more fuel-efficient models received a rebate. Cash for Clunkers proved wildly popular, quickly exhausting the $1 billion allocated for the program. Congress approved an additional $2 billion for the program. On the other hand, the $5 billion ARRA home weatherization program failed to meet its early goals, creating fewer jobs and weatherizing fewer homes than projected.

The Auto Industry Struggles

Even before Obama's inauguration, billions of dollars of TARP money had been handed out to stabilize the financial system. One of the major recipients of this first round of handouts, however, was not a financial institution. In the fall of 2008, auto industry executives from GM, Chrysler, and Ford approached the government for assistance. They needed a bailout to stay solvent. Like the bank bailout, the auto

U.S. auto industry executives request emergency financial aid during congressional hearings in 2008. Seen here are *(left to right)* GM Chairman Richard Wagoner Jr., Chrysler CEO Robert Nardelli, and Ford CEO Alan Mulally.

industry bailout was controversial with the public and some lawmakers, who believed that the automakers' own actions had brought about their financial problems.

During the 1990s and early 2000s, American automakers had begun focusing on the production of SUVs and large trucks, rather than smaller cars. The price of oil rose, however, and by 2008, American automakers' sales fell as consumers shopped for fuel-efficient vehicles. At the same time, the economic downturn further impacted sales. It became harder for potential car buyers to obtain credit, and people started to cut back on spending. Competition from foreign auto companies also became an issue, as the Japanese automaker Toyota began claiming a larger share of the U.S. auto market. U.S. automakers began losing money and were facing a possible collapse. Despite strong disapproval, Congress approved TARP bailout funds in late December.

Each automaker resolved its financial crisis differently. In March, the Obama administration forced the CEO of General Motors to resign. Two months later, the company filed for bankruptcy and reorganized, becoming smaller and, hopefully, more competitive. After distributing $50 billion to GM, the government took ownership of 60 percent of the company. Chrysler also accepted government assistance and declared bankruptcy. The company entered a new partnership with the Italian automaker Fiat. Ford opted against accepting government assistance; its decision was due to a 2006 restructuring plan that had protected the company from the full impact of the economic downturn. Ford returned to profitability in late 2009.

TARP Runs Its Course

In addition to the auto companies, a handful of the nation's largest banks—and the insurer AIG—accounted for the bulk of TARP money dispersed, each receiving more than $10 billion. Hundreds of smaller banks also received TARP funds. In early 2009, the recipients of large amounts of TARP funds underwent "stress tests" to check their financial soundness. Later in the year, many of the biggest banks began returning the government TARP funds. The Obama administration has also steered TARP money toward programs aimed to help homeowners facing possible foreclosure.

CHAPTER 3

ECONOMIC EFFECTS OF THE RECESSION

A s the recession grew worse in the months following the financial crisis, reporters and analysts often discussed what was happening on "Wall Street" versus "Main Street." Wall Street represented the financial industry and corporate culture, which many people blamed for the economic downturn. Wall Street's image was further damaged by the fact that numerous financial firms had handed out multimillion-dollar bonuses to top executives at the height of the crisis.

Main Street represented ordinary Americans worried more about their local economy than stock prices. As the bailout price tags grew, it seemed to some citizens that the government had overlooked the suffering experienced by the rest of the country. Main Street depends on a healthy financial industry, however, for loans to businesses and individuals. Even though people may resent corporate interests, corporate profits are an important driver of the economy.

THE RECESSION PERSISTS

As the recession progressed, the steady stream of bad economic news left both Wall Street and Main Street deeply concerned. In October

2009, some economists declared that the recession had ended. However, some important economic indicators took time to reflect the improving economic climate. Leading indicators, such as the stock market index, saw an improvement in the months before the recession ended. Lagging indicators, including the unemployment rate, continued to show the effects of the economic downturn. The GDP fell during three quarters of 2008 and during the first two quarters of 2009. The largest contraction occurred during the first quarter of 2009, a decline of 6.4 percent.

The Dow had reached an all-time high of 14,164 on October 9, 2007. On March 9, 2009, it closed at 6,547, its lowest point of the recession. During this decline, the stock market lost $11.2 trillion in value.

The price of gold surged during the recession, increasing to more than $1,000 per ounce from an average price of about $700 per ounce in 2007. The price of gold is significant because many people buy gold as a "safe" investment during times of economic uncertainty. A high demand for gold causes its price to rise.

The Consumer Confidence Index (CCI), which tracks people's outlook on the economy, also plummeted during the course of the recession. A number above 90 indicates that the economy is healthy, and a number above 100 shows solid growth. In July 2007, the CCI reached 111.9, the highest figure in nearly six years. By February 2009, the number had dropped to 25.3, the lowest point of the recession. Declines in consumer spending reflected this pessimism. The recession impacted manufacturing, and industrial production declined during 2008 and the first two quarters of 2009. New orders for goods—a

During an economic downturn, investors often turn to gold and other precious metals, such as silver and platinum. These are seen as safe investments that are unlikely to decline in value.

leading indicator—fell throughout 2008. During much of 2008, people's incomes declined as well.

THE EFFECTS OF PREDATORY LENDING

During the economic upswing before the recession began, millions of Americans achieved the dream of becoming homeowners for the first time. Many of these purchases were made possible by subprime mortgages. Lenders sometimes steered borrowers toward subprime loans, which offered high profits for banks, even when they would have qualified for traditional loans with better interest rates. Afterward, some lenders were accused of predatory lending, in which the borrower is not fully informed of the terms of the loan.

Home sales plummeted during the recession. According to the U.S. Census Bureau, new home sales had exceeded 1.2 million annually during the housing boom years of 2004 and 2005. By 2009, that figure fell to 374,000. In early 2010, sales of new homes hit the lowest level since 1963—the year record-keeping began for the statistic. The housing market was hit worse in some regions than others, especially in states such as California, Nevada, and Florida, which had seen huge housing growth before the recession.

The competitive housing market had caused a surge in the construction of new homes, also known as "housing starts." Housing starts are an important leading indicator. Housing starts reached a peak in early 2006 before declining drastically and maintaining a plateau for much of 2009 and 2010. The high number of foreclosed homes on the market discouraged new construction.

Foreclosures

Home foreclosure numbers soared due to the subprime mortgage crisis and the ensuing recession. More and more homeowners found themselves unable to afford their monthly mortgage payments. According to a 2010 article in *U.S. News and World Report*, 2.8 million properties were foreclosed in 2009, a new record. In 2010, there was little hope that the situation would improve quickly, since nearly 10 percent of mortgage holders were late on their payments. This indicated that foreclosure rates would continue to climb.

Foreclosures are devastating to owners who lose their home, but they can also affect local property values. Foreclosed homes, which revert to the ownership of the bank, are often poorly maintained and can eventually become an eyesore. In areas with high rates of foreclosure, this can drag down the entire neighborhood's property values.

Home prices declined about 30 percent from 2006 values during the recession. This became a major concern for people trying to sell their homes, some of whom had no choice but to accept offers of less than their original buying price. Declining values also affected mortgage holders. It became common for homeowners to owe more on their mortgage than the home was worth. In early 2010, about one in five mortgage holders had these "underwater mortgages." More and more people began deciding that it did not make financial sense to lose money by paying off underwater mortgages. They walked away from their homes, allowing them to be foreclosed. This trend has increased home foreclosure rates.

In March 2009, Obama introduced a $75 billion initiative to help keep people in their homes. It encouraged lenders to modify mortgages to make them more affordable. The program was not a huge success, reaching only a small proportion of struggling mortgage holders. A year later, Obama announced an expansion and new direction for the initiative. Part of the new effort aimed to prevent homes with underwater mortgages from going into foreclosure.

This foreclosed home is in La Mesa, California. In 2009, there were nearly two hundred thousand home foreclosures in California.

UNEMPLOYMENT

To many people, the persistent high unemployment rate has been the most devastating result of the recession. In December 2007, when the recession began, the unemployment rate was 5 percent, with 7.7 million people seeking jobs. In October 2009, the unemployment rate stood at 10.2 percent, with 15.7 million people out of work. This brought the unemployment rate to the highest level since 1983. About 8.4 million people lost their jobs during the course of the recession and the beginning of the recovery. From December 2008 to April 2009, more than half a million jobs were lost every month.

The high unemployment rate has not been the only concern. The length of unemployment for jobless workers is longer than during typical economic downturns. In early 2010, 6.3 million people had

UNDEREMPLOYMENT

Unemployment figures do not take into account underemployed or discouraged workers. Underemployed workers are those who are not working to their full capacity. For instance, these workers may have only part-time or temporary jobs. Discouraged workers are unemployed people who have given up on the job search due to the poor job market. They are also not counted in unemployment figures. According to the Bureau of Labor Statistics, it is estimated that, in early 2010, there were more than ten million underemployed and discouraged workers in the United States.

been unemployed for longer than six months. This was the highest level since the government began keeping record in 1948.

As with housing, the recession impacted the employment situation worse in some states than others. Michigan, with a heavy reliance on the auto industry, experienced the worst job loss, with the unemployment rate exceeding 14 percent. Nevada, Rhode Island, California, Florida, and South Carolina also saw unemployment rates significantly above the national average. North Dakota reported the lowest unemployment rates in the nation, with figures peaking at 4.4 percent. South Dakota and Nebraska also maintained unemployment rates well below the national average.

The American Recovery and Reinvestment Act was intended to combat unemployment by creating jobs and helping out-of-work Americans. The program saved jobs and prevented the unemployment rate from climbing even higher. However, it did not bring down the unemployment rate during its first year. Congress has renewed unemployment benefits several times since ARRA went into effect.

BREAKING NEWS • BREAKING NEWS • BREAKING NEWS • BREAKING NEWS • BREAKING NEWS • BREAKING

Michigan has attempted to reduce high unemployment rates by attracting new high-tech jobs to the state. Here, retrained workers and other job seekers wait in line to attend a 2009 Detroit job fair.

THE RECESSION HITS THE STATES

States often face fiscal difficulties for several years following the end of a recession. The ARRA helped states weather the initial crisis at first. Unfortunately for states, as the disbursements of ARRA funds began to taper off, it coincided with falling revenues brought about by the slow economy. Incomes, consumer spending, and property values all declined, leading to lower income taxes, sales taxes, and property taxes. Demand for state services such as Medicaid also grew due to the high unemployment rate, further straining state budgets.

As a result, some states are forced to choose between cutting back on services, raising taxes, or plunging into debt. Many state and city governments have had to lay off workers and take other cost-cutting steps. Some states have reduced their health care programs. Many states, wary of raising taxes during a recession, have increased various service fees. Cuts in education spending have impacted schools—Hawaii enacted a four-day school week in 2009—and led to steep increases in state college tuition rates. States have had little choice but to adapt to the economic downturn, but state and local cutbacks are a further hardship for many Americans still vulnerable from the recession.

CHAPTER 4

LIVING THROUGH THE RECESSION

Americans experienced hardships as the recession persisted. Jobless workers found that they were living off of unemployment checks instead of paychecks. Many people lost their homes or saw their home values decline. Workers took pay cuts. Some people saw the value of their investments shrink or lost their retirement savings as a result of the stock market downturn.

News stories reflected the hardships experienced by individuals and families. In between reports on economic indicators and statistics, there were profiles of laid-off workers and their difficulties in finding jobs. Food banks saw a spike in demand and a decline in donations. Some communities saw tent cities occupied by the homeless spring up on the outskirts of town. Children signed up for free school lunch programs in increasing numbers. More and more families began clipping coupons for the grocery store. The number of people filing for personal bankruptcy increased.

WIDE-RANGING EFFECTS

Not all Americans were impacted equally by the recession. Some career fields, such as construction, saw a greater spike in unemployment

than others. More men were laid off than women—partly because of the high number of jobs lost in manufacturing and the construction industry, areas that employ more men than women. Areas tradition- ally dominated by women, such as health care and education, better

Rural Colorado residents wait to pick up free food distributed by a food bank. The need for food aid, such as food pantry assistance and federal food stamps, has increased sharply during the recession.

withstood the recession. Young workers experienced very high unemployment, but older workers were also unemployed at higher-than-average rates. Enrollment rates increased at colleges and universities as people returned to school, hoping to improve their job prospects with additional education and training. Across the country, people were running up higher levels of personal debt at the beginning of the recession, while people's personal savings levels were plummeting.

Even those who managed to keep their jobs were affected by the recession. Many faced pay cuts or disruptions to their long-term career goals. Some workers stayed at a job during a time when they may have otherwise worked to advance their careers. People were less likely to take the risk of leaving their jobs during the recession, even if they disliked where they worked or wanted to try a new career field. Many workers accepted jobs that they were overqualified for.

Workers who find a job after a period of unemployment are generally relieved, but a new job does not automatically bring an end to financial hardship. They may still struggle with the financial consequences of the downturn, such as foreclosed homes or personal bankruptcies. Unemployment takes an emotional toll as well. Some jobless workers struggle with depression, anxiety, or troubled personal relationships as a result of the stress of unemployment.

Unemployment, especially extended periods of unemployment, often puts a serious strain on families. Losing a job can affect a person's sense of self-worth. It can also seriously impact family finances. The stress and conflict that results from this can have serious consequences. For instance, rates of domestic violence increase during recessions. Children are also more likely to suffer psychological disorders or struggle in school.

YOUNG WORKERS AND THE RECESSION

Young people, in particular, have been hit hard by the recession. In July 2009 (July is usually the peak period of employment for young workers), the unemployment rate stood at 18.5 percent among sixteen- to twenty-four-year-olds. This was the highest figure since 1948. Young adults also suffer more from extended periods of unemployment. With fierce competition for jobs, employers are more likely to hire new workers with solid work experience. For recent college graduates eager

BREAKING NEWS • BREAKING NEWS • BREAKING NEWS • BREAKING NEWS • BREAKING NEWS • BREAKIN

More than three thousand young people attend a youth job fair in Cincinnati, Ohio. Jobless rates during the recession were especially high for young adults, particularly low-income and minority youth.

to begin a career, a period of stagnation can permanently damage their career path. Young people entering the workforce during the recession of 1981–1982 earned significantly less than those starting out during brighter economic times.

Research has shown that a period of financial hardship during young adulthood can fundamentally change a person's outlook on life as well. Young workers who experienced such a period of time were more likely to accept safer jobs and stay at their jobs for longer stretches of time. Many of them tended to believe that the path to success depended more on luck than personal effort. Evidence even indicates that periods of unemployment can affect long-term mental and physical health, and these effects can be more pronounced on younger workers.

The Effect of the Recession on Older Workers

The recession has also derailed the plans of many older workers. Many workers nearing retirement age are not covered by traditional pension plans that provide a fixed monthly income. Instead, they put their savings in retirement investments such as 401(k) plans. These declined in value during the recession, leaving some older workers facing a devastating loss.

Financial circumstances have led some older workers to return to the workforce, where they often compete with younger people for jobs. Some older workers have been forced into retirement by layoffs. Others have been trapped by long-term unemployment. For older workers with a limited amount of time to rebuild their financial situation, an extended stretch of unemployment can cause them to slip below the poverty line.

LONG-TERM CONSEQUENCES

There has been much speculation on the long-term consequences of the recession. Previous recessions have generally left behind no permanent effects. Consumers return to their usual spending habits when the economy improves. However, some experts believe that this recession was so severe that it could have a lasting impact on American attitudes.

Many people who lived through the Great Depression emerged with a lasting sense of insecurity about money. After being forced to survive with very little, they developed a strict habit of living frugally. After

MOVING BACK HOME

The recession has brought many families together again—in the same home. Facing home foreclosures and high unemployment rates, an increasing number of people have decided that the financially sensible course of action would be to move in with relatives.

According to census data, nearly one out of five adults under thirty-five were living with their parents in 2008. Some move back after finishing college. Others "boomerang" back to their parents after living independently. Many are jobless or unable to afford their own place. Adults are getting married at a later age than in the past. Young people may delay marriage until they feel financially secure. For some young adults, this means living with parents for a longer period, especially when a recession gets in the way of prosperity. Also, more adults over sixty-five are moving in with their adult children. Many make the move for financial or health reasons.

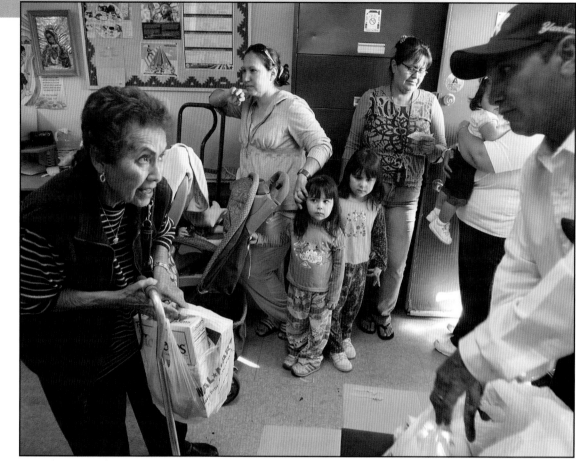

A volunteer distributes food to the needy in El Centro, California, in 2009. El Centro suffered from high unemployment, loss of construction jobs, and cuts in services due to a state budget crisis.

seeing banks fold and the stock market crash, these people developed a distrust of financial institutions.

The Great Depression was much more severe than the Great Recession. Still, many Americans today have re-evaluated their financial priorities. More people have vowed to increase the amount of money that they save. Many Americans lost trust in the stock market during the financial crisis. They indicate that they will wait to invest until the recovery is further under way or stop investing in the stock market altogether.

Even if Americans would prefer to return to their carefree spending habits, the post-recession economy may not allow it. Banks will not return to offering easy credit in the near future. Lasting high unemployment levels will prevent workers from taking their jobs—and prosperity—for granted.

CHAPTER 5

THE PATH TO ECONOMIC RECOVERY

Toward the end of 2009, economic indicators began to reflect an economic recovery. Stock prices began rising, and manufacturing orders and output have increased. Although the housing market was still fragile, home values stopped falling and even saw a slight increase. Consumer confidence and consumer spending edged up slightly. In the fourth quarter of 2009, the GDP grew at an impressive rate of 5.7 percent, although economists warned that the economy could not sustain such strong growth.

Still, many Americans feel left behind in the recovery. Unemployment levels remain high. Some analysts have asserted that there is an increasing divide between the fortunes of corporate America represented in the stock market and the lots of ordinary American workers. In early 2010, sales of luxury goods saw a healthy increase, while overall sales rose only slightly. Large companies were rebounding, while smaller businesses were still reeling from the credit crisis. This trend is disturbing, since small and mid-size companies supply the biggest share of jobs in the United States.

Some economists claimed that the government's interventions in the economy, including the ARRA and TARP, prevented an economic catastrophe. Other observers were more cautious in their praise, but it is generally agreed that the programs were a success. The ARRA saved jobs as the economy hit bottom and began to rebound. TARP funds stabilized the financial system. Despite outcry at the cost, the government lost less money in the bailouts than projected. It was expected that the government could lose several hundred billion dollars, but the actual figure may be less than $100 billion. During 2009 and 2010, Congress began debating new financial regulations that would prevent such a financial crisis from recurring. Obama also signed a new jobs bill in March 2010. The legislation aimed to spur hiring, and the president indicated that he hoped to follow up the bill with further job stimulus measures.

LOOKING TO THE FUTURE

As the economy stabilized, many Americans grew impatient to know what the future held, especially in terms of job growth. Economists described possible recovery scenarios in terms of the shape of the recession on a chart. A V-shaped recovery would be strong and fast. A U-shaped recovery would take longer. A W-shaped recovery would have a brief period of recovery, after which the economy would fall into a second decline before rebounding. An L-shaped recovery represents a period of stagnant growth that may include a "jobless recovery."

Economic indicators pointed to the likelihood of a steady recovery occurring much more slowly than people would prefer. It will

take time for the economy to recover, much less grow beyond pre-recession levels.

The recovery still faces some tough obstacles. Credit remains tight, which makes it difficult for individuals and businesses to make

Surrounded by members of Congress, President Obama signs the HIRE Act on March 18, 2010. The measure aimed to restore jobs by offering incentives such as tax benefits to employers.

investments that might encourage economic activity. Consumer spending is unlikely to rebound quickly. This is a bad sign for the recovery because increased consumer demand helped boost the economy out of previous recessions. The housing market is still troubled. The worst of the housing crisis is over, but it will take time for homes to regain value and even longer for unemployment in the construction industry to abate.

WAITING FOR JOBS

Unemployment began to level out in early 2010. In March, the economy added more than one hundred thousand jobs, the best report in about three years. Still, economists did not expect the unemployment rate to drop quickly. Many had predicted that the unemployment rate would not significantly decline until 2011.

About 8.4 million people lost their jobs during the recession. It is a good sign that the economy is no longer shedding jobs, but in order to reduce unemployment, the economy must create new jobs. To return to an unemployment rate of 5 percent, the economy would have to add ten million jobs. Even at a rate of five hundred thousand new jobs per month, accomplishing this would still take nearly two years. This rate of growth—five hundred thousand jobs per month—is wildly optimistic, however. Job growth will likely occur at a much slower pace. In addition, new workers are entering the job market at a rate of about 1.5 million a year. The economy must produce about an additional 125,000 jobs a month to accommodate these new workers.

Slow job growth will also affect the average income for American workers. With an unemployment rate near 10 percent, employers will not have a difficult time attracting new workers. They will not have to offer pay incentives when there is a wide pool of qualified workers eager to land a job. Workers may be less likely to push for pay increases when they could easily be replaced. As a result, it may take time for the recovery to bring about an increase in average incomes, which, in turn, will affect the overall economy.

UNKNOWN FACTORS

Before the housing market meltdown and financial crisis, few economists predicted the severity of the resulting recession. Likewise, there could be surprises in store that emerge during the recovery.

For example, troubles in the commercial real estate market could impact the recovery. Commercial real estate includes developments

BREAKING NEWS • BREAKING NEWS • BREAKING NEWS • BREAKING NEWS • BREAKING NEWS • BREAKIN

An employee walks through the Athens, Greece, stock exchange in April 2010 as the nation neared a financial crisis. Restoring economic stability to Greece will require massive governmental spending cuts.

REACHING GLOBAL MARKETS

In 2010, President Barack Obama announced a new initiative to double America's overseas exports within a span of five years. The plan was put forth as a means to help speed the recovery from the recession. Obama hoped that American producers could reach new global markets and create two million jobs. If American businesses could bring in more money from overseas exports, it could help spur economic activity.

such as office buildings, hotels, and apartment buildings.

As in the housing market, commercial real estate was booming before the recession. Since then, the value of commercial real estate has fallen. Owners are seeing higher vacancy rates and declining rents. The distressed commercial real estate market could lead to bankruptcies and foreclosures. This would hurt the banks that hold the loans and cities that depend on commercial real estate for revenue.

The recession didn't just affect the United States—it was a global economic downturn. Many countries saw their economies contract and unemployment levels rise. As a result, a number of governments enacted stimulus plans and bailed out their financial institutions. In early 2010, a financial crisis rocked the economy of Greece. The economic troubles threatened to affect the economic stability of the eurozone, which consists of the European countries that use the euro as currency. The crisis was resolved when the eurozone helped draw up a bailout plan for Greece. Nevertheless, Greece's crisis roiled the global economy and negatively impacted America's stock market. A larger international financial crisis could have a greater effect on the American economy.

National Deficits and Debt

The financial crisis in Greece was brought about by huge levels of national debt and deficit. Greece's national debt—the amount owed to outside creditors—was greater than its GDP. The nation's deficit—the amount that spending exceeds revenue—was more than 10 percent.

Greece's financial crisis left many Americans wondering if a similar scenario could occur in the United States. Increasing national debt and persistent budget deficits are a matter of concern to many economists and lawmakers. The stimulus plan and bailouts were both huge, expensive measures. In addition, government revenues fell during the recession while government spending increased, so the annual budgets also led to deficit spending. The United States has a significant national debt. In December 2007, when the recession began, the national debt was slightly higher than $9 trillion. By the end of 2009, it had passed $12 trillion—on its way to equaling the GDP, which is about $14 trillion.

The budget gap is filled by selling government securities, such as treasury bills, notes, and bonds to investors. Essentially shares of the national debt, these government securities are a very safe investment. The U.S. government has never failed to pay the interest owed on government securities. Banks, insurance companies, financial companies, and even private individuals buy up government securities. China and Japan each hold more than $700 billion in U.S. Treasury securities.

Critics claim that excessive government spending is endangering the future of the economy. In the long-term future, annual interest payments on the national debt will total hundreds of billions of dollars. As interest rates rise, these payments will become even more

Workers install a heating system in a Barre, Vermont, home in late 2009. The troubled housing market has stabilized as the economy has continued recovering from the recession.

expensive, potentially hampering economic growth. Others believe that stimulus spending and bailouts were necessary to rescue the economy from the brink of catastrophe. Deficits are undesirable but sometimes necessary, and the long-term growth made possible by strong intervention during the downturn will enable the economy to overcome the issue of the national debt in the future.

bailout The federal assistance given to failing companies during a recession.

bankruptcy The legal process by which an entity declares its inability to pay its debts.

business cycle Alternating periods of growth and contraction in the economy.

commodity Any bulk good, especially one that is largely unprocessed, that can be sold and traded.

competition In business, the rivalry between two parties for customers or markets.

consumer A person or organization that uses economic goods.

contraction A period of slowed economic activity.

corporation A legal entity, especially a business, that exists independently of its members. Corporations have rights, powers, and liabilities distinct from those of their members.

credit An arrangement to use or possess goods or services on condition of later payment.

debt Something that is owed.

deficit The amount by which a sum of money falls short of the needed amount.

depression A prolonged economic downturn marked by high unemployment levels.

exports Goods or services produced domestically and sold in foreign markets.

foreclosure The legal proceedings taken by a creditor to repossess a mortgaged property.

free market A financial market that is not subject to government intervention or regulation.

gross domestic product (GDP) The value of all goods and services produced by a nation in a year.

interest A sum paid or charged for borrowing money.

maverick A person who acts independently of others.

mortgage A pledge of property, such as a house, as security for a loan to be repaid under specific terms.

recession The economic downturn in the business cycle, usually defined as six months or more of declining GDP.

recovery The upward phase of the business cycle in which economic conditions improve.

stock Ownership shares of a company or corporation.

variable interest rate An interest rate that fluctuates, or changes.

Committee for a Responsible Federal Budget Project

1899 L Street NW, Suite 400

Washington, DC 20036

(202) 986-6599

Web site: http://www.stimulus.org

The Committee for a Responsible Federal Budget Project is a bipartisan and nonprofit organization that tracks stimulus funds and other government spending that were implemented to address the 2007 recession.

Conference Board

845 Third Avenue

New York, NY 10022-6679

(212) 759-0900

Web site: http://www.conference-board.org

This business membership and research organization tracks economic indicators and provides other services.

Department of Finance Canada

140 O'Connor Street

Ottawa, ON K1A 0G5

Canada

(613) 992-1573

Web site: http://www.fin.gc.ca

The Department of Finance oversees the Canadian government's budget and spending.

National Economists Club

P.O. Box 19281

Washington, DC 20036

(703) 493-8824

Web site: http://www.national-economists.org

The National Economists Club is a nonprofit organization dedicated to encouraging discussion and an exchange of ideas on economic trends and issues relevant to public policy.

U.S. Department of Commerce: Bureau of Economic Analysis

1441 L Street NW

Washington, DC 20230

(202) 606-9900

Web site: http://www.bea.gov

The Bureau of Economic Analysis is an agency that provides objective economic statistics to the public.

U.S. Department of the Treasury

1500 Pennsylvania Avenue NW

Washington, DC 20220

(202) 622-2000

Web site: http://www.treas.gov
The Department of the Treasury manages the finances of the U.S.
  government.

U.S. Securities and Exchange Commission
100 F Street NE
Washington, DC 20549
(202) 942-8080
Web site: http://www.sec.gov
This organization regulates investment in the United States.

WEB SITES

Due to the changing nature of Internet links, Rosen Publishing has
developed an online list of Web sites related to the subject of this book.
This site is updated regularly. Please use this link to access the list:

http://www.rosenlinks.com/hls/rece

FOR FURTHER READING

Acton, Johnny, and David Goldblatt. *Economy*. New York, NY: DK, 2010.

Berlatsky, Noah, ed. *The Global Financial Crisis*. San Diego, CA: Greenhaven Press, 2010.

Brancato, Robin F. *Money: Getting It, Using It, and Avoiding the Traps*. Lanham, MD: Scarecrow Press, 2007.

Clifford, Tim. *Our Economy in Action*. Vero Beach, FL: Rourke Publishing, LLC, 2009.

Craats, Rennay. *Economy: USA Past Present Future*. New York, NY: Weigl Publishers, 2009.

Downing, David. *Political and Economic Systems: Capitalism*. Chicago, IL: Heinemann, 2008.

Espejo, Roman. *The American Housing Crisis*. San Diego, CA: Greenhaven Press, 2009.

Flynn, Sean Masaki, Ph.D. *Economics for Dummies*. Hoboken, NJ: Wiley, 2005.

Gilman, Laura Anne. *Economics*. Minneapolis, MN: Lerner Publications, 2006.

Gross, Daniel. *Dumb Money: How Our Greatest Financial Minds Bankrupted the Nation*. New York, NY: Free Press, 2009.

Hall, Alvin. *Show Me the Money: How to Make Cents of Economics*. New York, NY: DK, 2008.

Hynson, Colin. *The Credit Crunch*. North Mankato, MN: Sea to Sea Publications, 2010.

Merino, Noel. *The World Economy*. San Diego, CA: Greenhaven Press, 2010.

Miller, Debra A. *The U.S. Economy*. San Diego, CA: Greenhaven Press, 2010.

Nagle, Jeanne. *How a Recession Works*. New York, NY: Rosen Publishing Group, 2009.

Orr, Tamra. *A Kid's Guide to Stock Market Investing*. Hockessin, DE: Mitchell Lane Publishers, 2009.

Riggs, Thomas, ed. *Everyday Finance: Economics, Personal Money Management, and Entrepreneurship*. Detroit, MI: Gale Group, 2008.

Tyson, Eric. *Investing for Dummies*. 5th ed. Hoboken, NJ: Wiley, 2008.

Wasik, John F. *The Audacity of Help: Obama's Economic Plan and the Remaking of America*. New York, NY: Bloomberg Press, 2009.

Whitcraft, Melissa. *Wall Street*. New York, NY: Children's Press, 2008.

BIBLIOGRAPHY

Aversa, Jeannine. "Jobless: 10 Percent Is Tougher Than It Used to Be." Associated Press, November 8, 2009. Retrieved April 1, 2010 (http://www.newsday.com/business/jobless-10-percent-is-tougher-than-it-used-to-be-1.1572219).

Epping, Randy Charles. *The 21st Century Economy: A Beginner's Guide.* New York, NY: Vintage Books, 2009.

Foroohar, Rana. "The Recession Generation." *Newsweek*, January 9, 2010. Retrieved April 2, 2010 (http://www.newsweek.com/id/229959).

Goodman, Peter S. "Despite Signs of Recovery, Chronic Joblessness Rises." *New York Times*, February 20, 2010. Retrieved April 2, 2010 (http://www.nytimes.com/2010/02/21/business/economy/21unemployed.html).

Luo, Michael. "Overqualified? Yes, but Happy to Have a Job." *New York Times*, March 28, 2010. Retrieved April 2, 2010 (http://www.nytimes.com/2010/03/29/us/29overqualified.html).

MacNeil/Lehrer Productions. "Unemployment Rate Holds Steady, but Minorities Still Worse Off." March 5, 2010. Retrieved April 2, 2010 (http://www.pbs.org/newshour/bb/business/jan-june10/jobs_03-05.html).

Mason, Paul. *Meltdown: The End of the Age of Greed.* New York, NY: Verso, 2009.

McNichol, Elizabeth, and Nicholas Johnson. "Recession Continues to Batter State Budgets; State Responses Could Slow Recovery."

Center on Budget and Policy Priorities, February 25, 2010. Retrieved April 2, 2010 (http://www.centeronbudget.org/cms/index.cfm?fa=view&id=711).

Mullins, Luke. "Strategic Defaults and the Foreclosure Crisis." *U.S. News and World Report*, January 19, 2010. Retrieved April 2, 2010 (http://www.usnews.com/money/personal-finance/real-estate/articles/2010/01/19/strategic-defaults-and-the-foreclosure-crisis.html).

Newman, Rick. "Why the 'Recovery' Is Taking So Long." *U.S. News and World Report*, April 2, 2010. Retrieved April 2, 2010 (http://www.usnews.com/money/blogs/flowchart/2010/04/02/why-the-recovery-is-taking-so-long).

New York Times. "Credit Crisis: The Essentials." January 12, 2010. Retrieved April 2, 2010 (http://topics.nytimes.com/top/reference/timestopics/subjects/c/credit_crisis/index.html).

New York Times. "Economic Stimulus." March 18, 2010. Retrieved April 2, 2010 (http://topics.nytimes.com/top/reference/timestopics/subjects/u/united_states_economy/economic_stimulus/index.html).

Peck, Don. "How a New Jobless Era Will Transform America." *The Atlantic*, March 2010. Retrieved April 2, 2010 (http://www.theatlantic.com/magazine/archive/2010/03/how-a-new-jobless-era-will-transform-america/7919).

Pugh, Tony. "Tight Job Market Is Squeezing Out Young Workers." McClatchy Newspapers, March 24, 2010. Retrieved April 2, 2010 (http://www.mcclatchydc.com/2010/03/24/90996/tight-job-market-is-squeezing.html).

Rugaber, Christopher S. "Two-Track Economy: 9.7% Unemployment, $200K Cars." Associated Press, March 18, 2010. Retrieved April 2, 2010 (http://finance.yahoo.com/news/Twotrack-economy-97-apf-670270394.html?x=0&sec=topStories&pos=main&asset=&ccode=).

Taylor, Paul, et al. "The Return of the Multi-Generational Family Household." Pew Research Center, March 18, 2010. Retrieved April 2, 2010 (http://pewsocialtrends.org/assets/pdf/752-multi-generational-families.pdf).

Tucker, Irvin. *Economics for Today*. 3rd ed. Mason, OH: Thomson Learning, 2003.

U.S. Bureau of Labor Statistics. Various data. Retrieved April 2, 2010 (http://stats.bls.gov).

Washington Post. "Timeline: Crisis on Wall Street." Retrieved April 1, 2010 (http://www.washingtonpost.com/wp-srv/business/economy-watch/timeline/index.html).

Wessel, David. "Wall Street Soars Above Main Street." *Wall Street Journal*, October 22, 2009. Retrieved April 2, 2010 (http://online.wsj.com/article/SB125616290488299949.html).

INDEX

ABOUT THE AUTHOR

Corona Brezina has written more than a dozen titles for Rosen Publishing Group. Several of her previous books have focused on current events and issues, including *Climate Change*, *Public Security in an Age of Terrorism*, and *Organ Donation: Risks, Rewards, and Research*. She lives in Chicago, Illinois.

PHOTO CREDITS

Cover Timothy A. Clary/AFP/Getty Images; pp. 4–5 Jim Watson/ AFP/Getty Images; pp. 7, 28–29 Bloomberg via Getty Images; pp. 9, 40 David McNew/Getty Images; pp. 12, 44–45 Mark Wilson/Getty Images; p. 14 Alex Wong/Getty Images; p. 17 Charles Ommanney/ Getty Images; pp. 20–21 Scott J. Ferrell/Congressional Quarterly/ Getty Images; p. 25 Kim Jae-Hwan/AFP/Getty Images; p. 31 Bill Pugliano/Getty Images; pp. 34–35 John Moore/Getty Images; pp. 37, 50-51 © AP Images; p. 47 Louisa Gouliamaki/AFP/Getty Images; interior graphics © www.istockphoto.com/Chad Anderson (globe), © www.istockphoto.com/ymgerman (map), © www.istockphoto.com/ Brett Lamb (satellite dish).

Photo Researcher: Peter Tomlinson